TAFTA:

The Agreement of the Strongest

Thomas Porcher - Frédéric Farah

TAFTA:
The Agreement of the Strongest

Max Milo
ESSAIS-DOCUMENTS

©Max Milo Éditions
Collection Essais-Documents, Paris, 2023
www.maxmilo.com
ISBN : 978-2-315-01264-0

Introduction

Today, in Brussels and the United States, a treaty is being signed that could radically change the lives of hundreds of millions of American and European citizens. The treaty does not yet have a fixed name, but a series of abbreviations and acronyms describe it: TAFTA (Transatlantic Free Trade Agreement), TTIP (Transatlantic Trade and Investment Partnership), GMT (Grand Marché Transatlantique)... It is a free trade agreement between the world's two largest economic zones, Europe and the United States. The aim is to lower trade barriers as much as possible — whether tariffs (customs duties) or non-tariff barriers (standards)— to facilitate trade between the two blocs.

According to the treaty's promoters, the economic chain would be virtuous: by removing these barriers, companies would find additional outlets, produce more goods and thus create jobs. Competition between companies would also enable consumers to obtain cheaper and more diversified goods, improving their purchasing power and offering them a wider choice of products.

But haven't we already heard this sweet melody when the single market was created? Our markets will certainly be more open, but will they create jobs? Will the new standards be European or American? And if the negotiators are multinational companies on both sides of the Atlantic, are they negotiating against each other, or are they agreeing to revise regulatory constraints and make them more permissive? Finally, will states still be able to set stricter standards once the treaty is ratified?

These are the questions this text seeks to answer. The task is a difficult one, given that the treaty is still being negotiated, and the information available is highly incomplete. But there are a number of elements that enable us to start thinking, even if it remains incomplete. Our approach already identifies a number of potential risks for consumers and workers, as well as for certain sectors of activity. It also shows that, with this agreement, the energy transition will be even more difficult to achieve.

In terms of gains for the public, the European Commission's forecasts for job creation and economic growth seem highly questionable. Conversely, by giving themselves the opportunity to redraw the boundaries of regulation, the gains for multinationals could be enormous.

The aim of this text is therefore to provide clear information to citizens on the effects that TAFTA could have, so that they take ownership of these issues and don't leave it to specialist committees to decide for them[1]. Because this treaty is everyone's business, given that the scope of the negotiations concerns the whole of our lives (food, education, health, social rights, etc.) and in no way responds to Europe's current problems, which are the need to combat unemployment, the ecological emergency or the regulation of finance. Let us no longer allow choices to be imposed on us in the name of the principles of an economic science that is all too often subservient to the interests of the strongest (multinationals, financial markets). Let us reject these deliberations behind closed doors and demand a genuine democratic debate.

---

1. Citizens' groups such as Stop TAFTA have already been set up in several regions.

TAFTA:
THE BEGINNINGS IN A NUTSHELL

The promotion of the Transatlantic Free Trade Agreement by the European authorities is part of a history that largely overlaps with that of the European Union. Indeed, free trade has been one of the basic principles of European integration, which has been strongly reflected in the creation of the single market, the single currency and the opening up of the European market to world trade.

European leaders have done their homework, so much so that today, the European Union is the area of the world least covered by tariffs[2]. However, this belief in free trade was largely manifested outside Brussels in the

---

2. In 2010, their average level was 2.2% on European products imported by the United States, and 3.3% on American products imported by the European Union.

GATT negotiating rounds[3], when EU leaders constantly emphasized the positive effects expected from further opening up of economies: more diversified, cheaper goods for consumers, and wider market opportunities for businesses. Well-known European Commissioners such as Peter Mandelson and Lord Leon Brittan have promoted this vision and, contrary to popular belief, the liberal doctrine is much more strictly applied in the institutions of the European Union than in the United States. Recently, in May 2014, José Manuel Barroso, in a speech at Stanford University, vigorously reaffirmed his belief in free trade[4].

As long ago as 2006, the European Union defined a trade policy strategy known as "Global Europe: Competing in the World"[5]. The aim of this strategy is to seek new-generation free-trade agreements with the European Union's main trading partners which, in addition to reducing customs duties, would extend their scope to all areas of trade and address behind-the-border barriers to trade: services, public procurement, protection of intellectual property rights, sustainable development, sanitary and phytosanitary standards. These agreements are referred to as "behind-the-border" agreements, because they deal with standards established within a country, rather than tariffs, which are a border-crossing fee.

---

3. GATT (General Agreement on Tariffs and Trade) is the forerunner of the World Trade Organization (WTO).
4. Barroso (José Manuel), "Global Europe, from the Atlantic to the Pacific," Stanford University, May 1, 2014, http://europa.eu/rapid/press-release_SPEECH-14-352_en.htm
5. European Commission, "Global Europe: Competing in the World", October 4 2006.

This trade strategy project has been translated into action, with an association agreement now in place with Peru and Colombia since May 2013, with Honduras, Nicaragua and Panama since August 2013, and with Canada since October 18, 2013. Other free-trade agreements with so-called "Eastern Partnership" countries are underway: Ukraine, Moldova, Georgia, Armenia, or negotiations with regional organizations such as the Gulf Cooperation Council or Mercosur[6].

The transatlantic partnership with the United States[7] is part of this strategy. From an institutional point of view, in 2009 the European Parliament voted almost unanimously for a resolution on transatlantic relations, calling for the construction of a truly integrated market by 2015. In January 2012, the Competition Directorate organized 135 meetings with various multinational companies to prepare for the upcoming negotiations. However, the negotiations really kicked off on January 8, 2013 and, to date, several rounds of negotiations have already taken place, with a conclusion envisaged during 2015[8].

---

6. Common market grouping together several South American countries.

7. The reality is that this partnership project has been in the drawer for over twenty years, but has gone through periods of slackness, notably between 1998 and 2005 (a period when the United States was trying to draw closer to China).

8. In order to exist, this treaty must undergo the two key stages provided for under international law: signature and ratification. Ratification will take place at European level, with Parliament voting in plenary session on the text resulting from negotiations between the Commission and the United States. It is important to note that the Parliament cannot amend the text, and that any veto

TAFTA: The Beginnings in a Nutshell

On the face of it, there's nothing to worry about, except that these objectives are in line with Europe's liberal policy. But a partnership with the USA will not have the same consequences as a partnership with Moldavia or Peru. Firstly, because, unlike other countries, Europe and the United States in the vast majority of cases engage in intra-industry trade, i.e. they exchange goods of the same type, which could increase competition and affect certain companies.

Secondly, because European goods are manufactured to different standards and under different conditions. This is where the treaty could become very worrying. How will this "approximation of standards" between the United States and Europe be achieved?

Finally, the treaty provides for the establishment of arbitration tribunals to guarantee investor protection. This legal mechanism deserves particular attention, as it essentially undermines the sovereignty of states. And it is to be feared that a private justice system will emerge, capable of condemning states and preventing the adoption of new, more protective laws.

And yet, according to the treaty's promoters, this partnership, by creating the world's largest free-trade zone, should create over two million jobs and generate over 3,000 billion in investment flows. Given the effects of the free-trade policies pursued in recent years, it's clear that these promises deserve careful scrutiny.

---

it may cast can be overridden by the Council. The Council plays a key role in the process, as it must unanimously adopt the decision to conclude the agreement; finally, the last stage takes place in the national parliaments, which will incorporate the provisions into the national law of each country.

Why Now?

The Greater Transatlantic Market project has been in the pipeline for more than twenty years, but has seen a marked acceleration since 2009. This acceleration of negotiations has taken place against a backdrop of global economic and geopolitical upheaval, with the rise of China and other emerging countries. But in this strategic alliance aimed at redefining global economic governance, Europe seems to be the pawn of the United States.

Since the end of the Second World War, governments have been trying to establish rules for international trade. To ensure that all countries are treated equally, the GATT established a number of principles: reciprocity, transparency and the most-favored-nation clause. Under this clause, when a country grants a favor, particularly a tariff, to another country, it grants the same to all countries trading with it, and foreign producers are subject to the same regulations as domestic producers.

The aim of the GATT, then the WTO[9], was clearly stated: to develop a framework to promote multilateralism.

But behind the fine principles of form and substance —transparent negotiations and the mobilization of as many countries as possible— multilateralism never took place. The rich countries often set the agenda for the negotiations and ensured that they emerged victorious in the haggling over the rules to be set. For example, they always agreed to liberalize technology-intensive sectors (because only they had the technology), and refused to open up sectors where they could face competition (agriculture and textiles).

The same rights do not mean the same opportunities. The multilateralism advocated by the GATT, then the WTO, does not erase the domination of the rich countries. You'd have to be very naive to think that Mali has as much power in negotiation rounds as the United States or the United Kingdom.

The reality is that if we consider Europe as a country, WTO negotiations were more like bilateral discussions. The figures bear this out: until the late 1980s, three-quarters of industrialized countries' trade was with other industrialized countries.

This façade of multilateralism, benefiting only a handful of countries, was disrupted by China's entry into the WTO in 2001. While most American and European leaders had supported China's entry, believing that their countries' exports would invade China, these countries' companies began to relocate to China.

---

9. In 1995, the GATT became the WTO, an institution with a dispute settlement body.

Other emerging countries, such as Brazil and India, are making their mark on international trade, and are no longer letting the Europeans or Americans impose the agenda on them in WTO negotiations[10], with the relative share of the USA and Europe weakening as a result. China has become the second economic power after the United States, and the two countries account for 19.2% of world exports[11].

It is against this backdrop that the USA is attempting to forge closer ties with China. However, despite their economic and financial interdependence, an agreement on production standards seems hopeless, given the differences in production processes. China is also an economic and military rival. The United States, beyond its unrivalled military budget[12], is developing a genuine commercial diplomacy. After the pactomania of the Cold War —i.e., military alliances to contain the USSR during this period— they want to promote a commercial pactomania: two huge treaties with the Pacific and European powers to contain China.

But it was not in the interests of US multinationals that the Trans-Pacific Treaty should be signed before the Transatlantic Treaty. Indeed, the Pacific countries generally have production and consumption standards

---

10. For example, on July 31, 2014, India vetoed the Bali agreement sealed in December 2013 and supposed to facilitate customs procedures between the 160 WTO member states. It would have agreed to sign it if progress had been made on another text allowing it to continue subsidizing its agriculture.
11. WTO (2012).
12. The US military budget is equivalent to that of all the other countries in the world.

that are less restrictive than American standards (negotiations generally focus on lowering the constraint of standards, as before, on lowering tariffs, not raising them). Successful negotiations with Pacific Rim countries, through the introduction of less restrictive standards, would have led major American companies to adjust to Pacific Rim standards, and to bear the costs of this adjustment.

So we have to start with Europe. Because the establishment of common standards (consumer and production standards) between the USA and Europe will make them global standards, including for the Pacific, including for China. The transatlantic market will thus be the producer of global standards. It will then be possible for the US government, under pressure from US corporate lobbies, to negotiate with Pacific Rim countries without having to lower its regulations —which will now apply to all countries— and thus without any major changes to US production techniques. The major companies in the industrial countries of the Pacific will then have to adapt their techniques, or risk being excluded from the European and American markets.

The United States therefore called Europe back for a new round of negotiations, and Europe, which seemed to have missed its chance to play an international role commensurate with its economic weight, returned to center stage, albeit in spite of itself.

Deceptive Transparency

One of the most frequently voiced criticisms of TAFTA is its lack of transparency. According to NGOs and citizens' groups, negotiations are opaque and disregard the rights of citizens and elected representatives. Paradoxically, the Brussels Commission has developed an intense communication campaign on the treaty and the various rounds of negotiations. It has set up a website accessible in all languages, containing numerous documents on Brussels' positions and the negotiating timetable. The negotiators are also supported by a council of experts comprising business representatives and civil society associations, while the most controversial provisions of the treaty —such as arbitration tribunals— are the subject of a Europe-wide online consultation[13]. Finally, the ratifi-

---

13. The consultation ran from March 27 to July 31, 2014. Exactly 149,399 responses were received. Austria, Germany and Sweden in

cation of the treaty, i.e. its incorporation into French law, should involve both the European Parliament and national parliaments. With so much concern for communication, consultation and involvement of European and national parliamentarians, can we still speak of opacity in the TAFTA negotiations? Unfortunately, yes, because this transparency is illusory for several reasons.

First of all, the information on the Brussels Commission's website is vague. It is little more than a collection of speeches and assertions, devoid of figures and reflection, whose sole aim is to reassure the reader. The answers to the questions are nothing more than a series of banalities, such as "the economic growth and increased productivity created by the agreement will benefit workers in the Union and the United States", or "the aim of the partnership will not be to make commercial profits at the expense of the health of our consumers", or "we will not compromise existing levels of protection to reach an agreement[14]", without mentioning the implementation of concrete studies capable of answering questions such as: "How will this standardization of standards be achieved? On what timescale? Or, "Given that the United States has not ratified the Kyoto Protocol, will it be possible to introduce regulations to combat global warming once

---

particular took part in the consultation. France's participation was relative, with 9,791 responses. The results and conclusions will be presented by the Brussels Commission in November 2014.

14. European Commission website: "Frequently asked questions (TTIP)", http://ec.europa.eu/trade/policy/in-focus/ttip/questions-and-answers/index_fr.htm

the treaty is signed?" Putting information online in no way guarantees greater transparency, or even better access to the public. The facts bear this out: while the gestation of the treaty began in 2009 with a near-unanimous vote by the European Parliament, five years on, the citizens of European countries know little or nothing about the negotiations. Why not? Because the negotiations are taking place in private, without them or their elected representatives, even though the treaty is likely to profoundly alter the way they work and consume.

As for online consultation, this in no way guarantees greater transparency. In the past, we used to leave blank notebooks for local residents to express their opinions on a project; today, we're opening an online consultation at European level. But what will the Commission do with all these opinions? Will it include them in an appendix to the final treaty, or will it simply note that an online consultation with thousands of reactions was taken into account in setting up the mechanism for arbitration tribunals? The consultation only serves to gather opinions to justify that the process remains democratic, but nothing will change. In fact, there was never any question of abolishing arbitration tribunals, only of gathering opinions.

And even if there were to be a genuine democratic debate with a vote by universal suffrage, history shows that many European texts have been rejected in referendums, only to resurface in barely modified form. In France, for example, the 2005 referendum on the European Constitutional Treaty resulted in a 54.68% "no" vote. The vote was democratic, but that didn't stop France from ratifying it, bypassing the will of the majority of the French people.

But the greatest democratic danger lies in the agreement itself, as it is intended to incorporate the Anglo-Saxon legal technique of a Living Agreement, i.e. a living agreement which does not find its final point in signature and ratification, as it is destined to evolve. Under these conditions, it is possible to imagine that an a minima agreement will be presented initially to reassure the public, and that negotiations will then continue in opacity.

UNITED STATES VS. EUROPE: WHO IS STRONGER?

Some promoters of the treaty claim that Europe is in an economically strong position vis-à-vis the United States. In an article entitled "Traité transatlantique: le plus gros risque serait de ne pas conclure[15]", Vincent Champain, member of the "mondialisation" group at the Observatoire du long terme, points out that the European Union has a GDP of $16,400 billion, compared with $15,700 billion for the United States, and that the balance of trade between the two zones is $125 billion in Europe's favor. Given these figures, the Europeans can look forward to the negotiation rounds with confidence. However, a closer analysis of Europe's economic and operational data reveals a very different reality.

---

15. Champain (Vincent), "Traité transatlantique: le plus gros risque serait de ne pas conclure", La Tribune, April 28, 2014.

Firstly, with regard to GDP comparisons, it should be noted that the European Union has a population of 502 million, compared with 314 million in the United States, so that GDP per capita —which is a more relevant indicator— is around 40% lower. Added to this is the heterogeneity of the European Union in terms of GDP per capita[16]. For example, Germany's is only 21% lower than that of the United States, compared with 30% for France, 36% for Italy and 68% for Romania[17].

Secondly, in several key economic sectors, the European Union has completely fallen behind its American rival. For example, in the ranking of the top ten consumer electronics companies, there is not a single European company, compared with six American ones. The same applies to IT and financial services, where the top three places are held by American companies. Finally, the ranking of the ten most powerful brands in the world attests to the dominance of the United States, with eight companies ranked, while no European company appears on the list[18].

Thirdly, Europe's political weakness in the face of the United States. Whereas the European institutions were supposed to show a strong Europe with a stable president and a high-level representative, it now has no less than five presidents: a stable presidency, a rotating presidency, a president of the Parliament,

---

16. Calculated in purchasing power parity.
17. Borey (Grégoire), Chantrel (Étienne), "L'Union européenne une puissance économique 'unie dans la diversité'", in La France dans l'Union européenne, INSEE Références, 2014 edition.
18. Best Global Brands 2013, Interbrand ranking.

a president of the Eurogroup and a president of the European Commission. Yet these five presidents do not reflect a clear form of leadership. The European Union is fragmented and does not express a common sovereignty; it is merely the sum of economically and politically divergent states. But 28 sovereignties do not add up to one.

This difference is reflected in the economic policies pursued by the two groups. Whereas, contrary to popular belief, the United States is pragmatic in its use of fiscal and monetary policy to boost economic growth, Europe has imposed rigid dogmas (balanced budgets, anti-inflation policies) that deprive it of the economic policy levers that everyone else uses (China, the United States and Japan in the first instance), and have led it to play a game of "watch the bad guys".

But because these rules are ill-suited to Europe's heterogeneous nature, imposing the same constraints on countries with different demographic and economic dynamics, they give rise to endless internal divisions and debates. In the end, rather than looking outwards with a determination to impose itself on the world, as the United States does, Europe is undermined from within and turned in on itself.

Just compare the way the USA and Europe use their currency. While Europe remains obsessed with the link between monetary policy and inflation, the United States uses the dollar as a weapon to subsidize its exports. By devaluing their currency, the Americans improve the competitiveness of their exports. On the other hand, thanks to devaluation, imports from Europe appear more expensive in the United States,

United States vs. Europe: Who is Stronger?

which, conversely, increases the competitiveness of American domestic products.

So why don't Europeans do the same and devalue the euro? Once again, the problem lies in the economic heterogeneity of European countries. The high level of the euro puts some countries at a disadvantage, while benefiting others, as Louis Gallois rightly reminds us: "The strong euro strengthens the strong and weakens the weak; it favors those who have managed to escape price competition by positioning themselves at the top end of the market[19]." As the balance of power also exists within Europe, the euro has appreciated by over 60% since 2001.

In the context of the transatlantic market, manipulation of the dollar and standardization of standards would give a huge advantage to American multinationals, since US-European trade is intra-industry trade[20], and could only be in favor of the United States, since the fall in the dollar would make American goods cheaper than those of Europeans. Worse still, as the majority of trade is intra-European, American exports —cheaper and now possible thanks to the standardization of American and European standards— could replace those of certain European countries, resulting in a loss of outlets for companies in these countries[21].

---

19. Tenoux (Jean-Pierre), "Interview with Louis Gallois", l'Est républicain, February 22, 2013.

20. Trade in similar goods.

21. Today, standards are virtually the only barriers to trade between the USA and Europe. By lowering standards, the U.S. gains a competitive advantage by manipulating the dollar. European companies that trade with each other free of standards could find

Finally, Europe is more liberal than the United States. Indeed, since its inception, Europe has attempted to standardize economic and social models specific to each country, by promoting liberalization through the market. Contrary to popular belief, the European Union is far from being the home of social rights, or even a bulwark against the market economy. Admittedly, at the outset, because of the heterogeneity of companies, sectors and markets, it was torn between a more interventionist path and one more confident in the market, but since then it has undergone a transformation, hastily embracing the paths of an obsessive liberalism that reveres competition. In the face of unbridled financialization and speculation, it has offered a currency that has been no more than a glass shield; in the face of its inhabitants' concerns about junk food at work on our plates, it has shown itself at times complacent about GMOs and revived the nightmare of animal meal, which has been reintroduced since June 2014! The reality is that TAFTA is nothing more than an extension, thirty years on, of the single market, and we're a long way from the simplistic opposition that would turn Europe into the Gallic village besieged by the American empire. In economic terms, the European Union, far from being a protective shield, is the transmission belt for globalization and its deleterious effects.

In these conditions, where in Europe as in the United States, the State's mission is no longer to contain the

---

themselves in fierce competition with their American counterparts once standards are lowered.

market but to increase its strength, it is clear that the interests of industry will be at the heart of the negotiations and that industrial lobbies will shape this treaty. The figures speak for themselves: for example, the financial industry has 700 lobbying organizations at European level and spends 123 million euros a year, while NGOs and consumer associations have a budget of just four million[22].

However, lobbies of competing companies easily agree when the interests of their principals converge. If it's a question of lowering standards to make more profit, competing brands are capable of acting together. Remember how the chocolate industry lobbies succeeded in getting the European Parliament to accept a reduction in the proportion of cocoa (by replacing it with vegetable fats costing three to ten times less) while retaining the designation of chocolate[23]. In this case, the big loser is the consumer. TAFTA is certainly a way of pitting European and American industries against each other, but it is above all a tool used by multinationals against the interests of European and American citizens.

---

22. NGO Corporate Europe Observatory.
23. Chavagneux (Christian), "Chocolat beurk", Alternatives économiques, n° 180, April 2000.

STANDARDS AT STAKE

Standards are at the heart of the transatlantic treaty negotiations. The list of these standards is long, as it covers vast areas of our daily lives, whether in terms of health, food or intellectual property. It's a sensitive subject that has been the subject of controversy for a number of years, not only in transatlantic relations, with famous cases such as hormone-treated chicken, but also within Europe. We remember the divergent positions of European countries on place-of-origin labelling on products[24]. The question is whether the transatlantic treaty, by establishing common standards, will lead to a levelling down of standards?

---

24. Coldiretti, an association of Italian farmers, denounces the lowering of food standards by the European authorities, since it is not compulsory to indicate the place of origin on the label of certain products. According to the association, 29 million kilos of tomato concentrate arrived without a label.

For the treaty's promoters, these standards carry an ambiguity: they are certainly the expression of a concern to ensure consumer citizens a certain level of safety in various fields, but they are also a means of more subtle protection against competitors. For if certain products do not comply with precise rules, which are sometimes costly to respect, they cannot cross borders. There are a number of examples to support this argument, but they should not obscure the many times when citizens' choices far outweigh the economic considerations of industrialists. Banning hydraulic fracturing in France is in no way a means of protecting ourselves from any competition; it is first and foremost a societal choice. And it is to be feared that the TAFTA negotiations will put many of our choices back on the table (ban on GMOs, hydraulic fracturing, etc.) because they are seen by some as barriers to competition.

First of all, it's important to understand that the term "standard" covers several meanings, with varying degrees of implication for citizens[25]. Some standards are technical, while others are more concerned with sanitary or phytosanitary issues, and the aim of the treaty would be to bring these standards closer together in order to define common production and consumption standards between Europe and the United States.

For the treaty's promoters, this would simplify trade, since different standards often mean that production has to be adjusted to suit different countries, thus

---

25. According to the WTO definition: "Technical regulations and standards set out the specific characteristics of a product, such as its size, shape, design, functions and properties of use, or the way in which it is labeled or packaged before being offered for sale."

generating additional costs for companies. On this point, the treaty would simply amplify an earlier agreement on the recognition of certification bodies[26]. A number of companies are pushing in this direction, such as automakers on standards for seatbelts and other vehicle components. According to their promoters, the treaty would enable "this approximation of standards", which would benefit businesses.

This line of reasoning is extremely naive, as there will be no rapprochement, but rather an adjustment of the standards of one of the two parties. In other words, the companies of one party will have to adjust to the standards of the other, and the costs of this adjustment will be borne solely by one of the two parties. Particularly when it comes to technical standards, how can we seriously envisage a rapprochement on the size of a refrigerator cable or seatbelts? In this type of situation, history shows that the adjustment is always made to the standards of the strongest or the least restrictive. In some sectors, such as the automotive industry, European companies may be in a strong position to impose their standards, but in others, such as mass retailing, where seven American companies rank among the world's top ten companies in terms of sales, the cost of adjusting standards will be borne by European companies.

Under these conditions, a free-trade agreement is in fact the agreement of the strongest, since weaker competitors are relegated to the role of followers, obliged to adjust to the leader's technical standards

----

26. A European producer must always comply with American standards through an accredited European organization.

Standards at Stake

and to bear the cost (which will further strengthen the position of the strongest).

But this bickering over technical standards hides the heart of the matter: sanitary and phytosanitary standards. The treaty's promoters deliberately confuse the two, while technical standards on the length of a refrigerator cable do not have the same consequences for consumers as lowering food specifications.

In fact, it is on this point that differences are greatest, as they affect risk assessment and collective lifestyle choices. These standards, designed to protect the consumer, represent costs for companies. Just as American and European companies have diverging interests in technical standards, because they do not want to bear the cost of adjustment, their interests in health standards can converge to lower their level of protection. For example, on issues such as the ban on hydraulic fracturing in France or Bulgaria, Total and Exxon —despite being competitors— have a common interest: changing or repealing the law. When it comes to increasing their profits by making legislation less restrictive, multinationals —be they competitors, American or European— generally speak with one voice.

It's clear that the transatlantic treaty will provide an opportunity for manufacturers to reopen debates on bans, and then to take countries with the strictest legislation to arbitration tribunals. And many products will be the subject of debate in the food sector, such as chicken rinsed with chlorine solutions, hormone-treated beef or pork fed with ractopamine[27].

---

27. A drug that boosts lean meat content.

Some will tell you that Americans eat these products, and that tourists to the U.S. don't take special precautions when eating out. For the promoters, it's important to get away from the fantasy of the big bad American or the idea that Europe has stricter health standards than the United States. In fact, French cheese is banned in the United States, as is foie gras from intensive force-feeding. But that's not the problem, it's the right of a community to choose its way of life, whereas the essence of TAFTA is to place the principle of free market access above collective cultural preferences. Under these conditions, banning a product fed with GMOs could be considered a distortion of competition.

This is why the Brussels Commission is developing a communication to reassure the European consumer. For example, on February 18, 2014, European Commissioner Karel De Gucht asserted that "it is necessary to find a legal compromise between the need for public policies to protect individuals and the environment, and, on the other, to protect and encourage investment and its corollaries: jobs and growth[28]".

But this statement can only heighten concerns, and attests to the contradictions in the construction of TAFTA. Firstly, while the Commission is constantly reaffirming that consumer choice will be respected, there is talk of compromising on standards deemed too protective. This in itself is unacceptable. Secondly,

---

28. Cf. "Stepping Up a Gear: Press Statement by EU Trade Commissioner Karel De Gucht following the stocktaking meeting with USTR Michael Froman on the Transatlantic Trade and Investment Partnership (TTIP)", European Commission, Statement, Washington, February 18, 2014.

Standards at Stake

it confirms the opposition between protecting citizens and the environment on the one hand, and multinational investment on the other. And since the TAFTA negotiations are taking place in complete opacity, and above all bypassing the democratic process, we find ourselves in an absurd situation where two stakeholders (citizens-consumers-workers and corporations) are at odds over choices, while only the components of one party (the corporations) have the right to negotiate with each other. Under these conditions, talk of compromise is hypocritical.

And what if states, responding to the wishes of their citizens, refuse to lower standards or enact new protective standards? Multinationals could then take their case to arbitration tribunals and have these states condemned to pay heavy fines. The trap is closing.

Speculation on Job Creation

The TAFTA treaty, like many other free-trade agreements before it, claims massive job creation. European Commissioner Karel De Gucht puts the figure at two million jobs. The basic idea is that Europe and the United States, two major trading blocs, could offer each other new outlets for their industries by reducing non-tariff barriers. But both the figure and the method are open to criticism, and a brief flashback to the serenades of free trade in the European single market and the North American Free Trade Agreement (NAFTA) suggests caution.

As far back as 1988, the Cecchini report[29] on "the costs of non-Europe" praised the single market of 1986, promising Europeans millions of extra jobs

---

29. Cecchini (Paolo) (ed.), "Une évaluation des effets économiques potentiels de l'achèvement du marché intérieur de la communauté européenne", Économie européenne, no. 35, March 1988.

and economic growth of up to 6.5% a year. Today, the results of the single European market largely temper the enchanted vision of the Cecchini report: European growth has never taken off, and the unemployment rate has remained at the same level, before deteriorating sharply with the economic crisis.

In 1994, the North American Free Trade Agreement (NAFTA) promised growth, job creation and a narrowing of the income gap between the USA and Mexico. In retrospect, however, the NAFTA's record on job creation is poor, to say the least. A study by the Economic Policy Institute reveals that the United States lost over a million jobs between 1993 and 1999. Mexico, meanwhile, is said to have lost around a million jobs in corn cultivation[30]. Finally, the study also shows that income inequalities have increased, collective bargaining capacities have weakened and the impact on wages has been negative.

So how do we explain these discrepancies between forecasts and facts? One explanation can be found in the analysis of the forecasting models that led to the figure of "two million jobs". Four studies were commissioned by the Brussels Commission to assess the economic impact of the treaty: Ecorys (2009), CEPR (2013), CEPII (2013), Bertelsmann/ifo (2013). They form the scientific basis for promoting the agreement. Of the four studies, only one forecasts the creation of two million jobs (Bertelsmann/ifo). Incidentally, these

---

30. Scott (Robert E.), "The high price of 'free' trade: NAFTA's failure has cost the United States jobs across the nation", Economic Policy institute, November 17 2003.

jobs are not created in Europe alone, but in all OECD countries. The other three studies do not assess job creation, as the economic model used does not allow them to do so, due to an intrinsic assumption that the economy is already at full employment! In fact, the authors analyze only the effects on GDP, wages or exports, on the assumption that they would lead to job creation.

These studies use economic models that are impressive to the uninitiated (and even to the initiated) because they are made up of large systems of equations that are complex to solve. It is these lines of equation which, in the eyes of citizens and politicians alike, give the results obtained their legitimacy. A figure requiring such complexly resolved models can only be "sacred" and therefore difficult to question. However, for those who are not impressed by the equations, behind the facade of the model lie extremely simplistic and often implausible operating assumptions. Yet it is these assumptions that determine the final forecast.

Let's take the example of the Ecorys, CEPII and CEPR studies. They use the GTAP and Mirage models. In economics, these are a class of models known as "computable general equilibrium models". One of the assumptions of these models is the aggregation of all individual behaviors into a representative agent. Economically speaking, this agent, supposed to represent the heterogeneity and complexity of individual behavior in the United States and Europe, is guided in life solely by its "calculator" function, since it must, according to the assumption, maximize its utility under the constraint of a budget. In these models, only prices interest him; tastes and product quality don't count. And so, for example, a reduction in protection against chlorinated chicken or GMOs can have beneficial effects on the economy, since lower standards lead to lower prices and thus to greater consumption of these products by the representative agent.

However, more concrete studies of consumer behavior in 2013 show that they are shunning clever products (sales, competitive prices, etc.) and taking refuge in simple, sustainable values[31]. Clearly, consumer behavior in the USA and Europe is far more heterogeneous and complex (mood, fashion, etc.) than the representative agent hypothesis used in these models.

Bernard Guerrien, Ph.D. in economics and mathematics, calls any representative agent approach "an aberration" and "absurd". He also describes computable general equilibrium models as "fables", which can be adapted to suit the policies we wish to promote[32].

Alongside the assumptions specific to the model's operation, there are the assumptions made by the authors concerning the causal link between the variables (how the variables should be related to each other) and the analysis period. With regard to the causal link, the authors of the studies assume a 25% reduction in non-tariff barriers and a 100% reduction in tariff barriers, in order to measure the impact on US and European GDP, exports, wages and employment. But therein lies the double discourse surrounding the

---

31. CREDOC/PAIR Conseil, "April 8, 2013 press release", Les Cahiers de la consommation.
32. Guerrien (Bernard), Dictionnaire d'analyse économique, Paris, La Découverte, 4th ed., 2012, p. 197.

TAFTA negotiations: on the one hand, we are assured that there will be no lowering of standards, and on the other, we are promised job creation and growth provided there is a 25% reduction in non-tariff barriers. For the authors, there is a link between lower standards and economic gains. And with a 25% reduction in non-tariff barriers, sanitary and food standards will have to be cut to the bone. It's also worth noting that, while the reduction in non-tariff barriers is high on the one hand, the results in terms of growth are quite low, even in the most optimistic scenarios: 1.31% increase in GDP over the long term for Europe, and for the majority of studies the gain is less than 1%.

With regard to the analysis period (which determines the term of the forecast), with the exception of the Ecorys study, all the models are based on long-term forecasts, of at least ten years. In this case, the study predicting the creation of two million jobs has a time horizon of ten to twenty years. In other words, TAFTA, even if it had positive effects on employment, does nothing to address the urgent problem of Europe's 25 million unemployed.

To this we must add the fragility of long-term forecasts, which are based on an extremely conventional evolution of the world (all parameters are constant) and neglect medium- and short-term adjustment costs. For example, the models do not consider any possibility of changing policies or parameters. They forecast constant policies, legal rules and behavior.

Yet history shows that there can be surprises (even when they weren't so unforeseeable). For example, in the early 2000s, no long-term forecast took into account

Speculation on Job Creation

the subprime crisis or the rise of the emerging countries. Yet these structural changes have turned forecasts on their head, particularly in terms of employment, growth, debt and commodity prices.

In the final analysis, for the forecast of two million jobs, like the impact on growth or exports, to come true, a number of conditions must be met[33]. Firstly, that the models' assumptions, like those adopted by the authors, match reality —which, as we saw earlier, seems unlikely— and secondly, that there are no surprises to disrupt the forecast, i.e. that it is made according to the famous formula "all other things being equal". In the real world, these forecasts are unlikely to come true, and it's easy to see why the economic forecasts for Europe's single market or NAFTA were so far from reality. Because, all too often, economic reasoning is not used to inform policy but only to legitimize it; as in our case, where these studies are first and foremost ideological weapons to promote TAFTA.

---

33. A study by OFSE (Österreichische Forschungsstiftung für internationale entwicklung) entitled "Assessing the Claimed Benefits of the Transatlantic Trade and Investment Partnership (TTIP)", published in March 2014, also finds price elasticities too high (by a factor of two) compared with models traditionally used in economic literature. Price elasticities characterize the behavior of consumers and producers as a function of price movements, in particular the fact that a fall in prices necessarily leads to more consumption. However, by adopting very high price-volume elasticities, the authors deliberately amplify the virtues of free trade by assuming that consumers and producers are highly sensitive to falling prices.

A Treaty that Impedes Energy Transition

In the energy sector, the Transatlantic Energy Treaty has the same objectives as in other sectors: trade liberalization, the elimination of trade barriers (tariff and non-tariff) and investor protection. For the treaty's promoters, the liberalization of energy markets would lead to lower prices, which would benefit consumer purchasing power and industrial competitiveness. It would also make it possible to diversify supply sources in Europe, notably by replacing Russian gas with American shale gas. Finally, by promoting trade, the transatlantic market would stimulate innovation and enable technology transfer, which would benefit the development of renewable energies and thus promote the energy transition. Unfortunately, these arguments, which extol the virtues of liberalization as an objective truth, are in reality designed to bolster the current position of the multinational energy companies.

Firstly, the structure of energy production and consumption is highly rigid and inert. This is because entry costs are high due to the infrastructure required —you don't open an oil company like you would a grocery store— and demand is not very price-elastic — you don't change your car or heating system according to the price of energy. These specific features make the sector oligopolistic. Just look at the consequences of energy liberalization in the UK in terms of pricing and market structure. Even though it was considered by the European Commission as the example to follow, the liberalization of the British electricity market has resulted in an oligopoly of six companies sharing the market in the absence of any credible competitive threat[34]. Naturally, electricity prices have risen, just as they were supposed to. This is a far cry from the forecasts made by the European Commission's experts when the single market was created.

The opening of the transatlantic market will probably lead to a similar situation, with a relatively limited number of majors, already well known, sharing the various markets without anyone getting involved in a price war. With the integration of the American and European gas markets, gas and coal prices could even rise[35].

---

34. Boroumand (Raphaël Homayoun), "La dame de fer, la main invisible et la fée électricité", Le Monde, July 15, 2013.
35. The integration of the American and European gas markets could lead to higher gas prices, which would have an impact on the price of coal. Currently, the price of gas in the United States is

The other argument is that renewable energies will develop thanks to the innovations brought about by trade and technology transfer. Once again, this sequence reveals an enchanted vision of the market economy. Most innovations are not born of economic liberalism; they are the fruit of public policies of investment in research. Even the Internet is not the result of entrepreneurial dynamism, and would never have existed without years of public research by the US Department of Defense. Similarly, South Korea's transformation from an economy exporting low-end products to a world power in the automotive and steel sectors is above all the result of political choices, and not of mechanisms generated naturally by market forces.

In fact, ten years ago, some economists were arguing that, as oil prices rose, the energy transition would naturally get underway. The basic idea was that rising oil prices would make renewable energies more profitable, and thus enable them to enter the market. Once again, history has shown the opposite: the price of oil has risen fivefold in ten years, without renewable energies gaining a significant foothold. It's clear that without political will, there will be no development of

---

around four dollars, compared with eleven dollars on the European market. American companies are looking to export their gas to Europe. However, as the cost of transporting gas is high, it is likely that the price of gas will not fall in Europe. On the American side, gas exports will crowd out part of the supply destined for Americans, and the price of gas in the US will rise as a result. Americans could then substitute coal for gas again, just as they did with coal when gas was relatively cheaper, and coal prices could rise in turn.

renewable energies, and the transatlantic market will only consolidate the power of existing industries for decades to come.

Finally, we note bitterly that one parameter is absent from the negotiations, and yet directly linked to energy: the climate constraint. And yet, on a global scale, some 80% of our energy consumption is fuelled by polluting energies: oil, coal and gas. Throughout the 20th century, these energies were mainly consumed by OECD countries, which are responsible for two-thirds of CO_2 emissions despite accounting for just 15% of the world's population. Yet the most violent impacts of climate change are felt by the populations of the southern hemisphere, where seasons and temperatures affect crop yields and fishing. Some are already suffering the consequences of our lack of action, and in 2012 there were over 32 million climate refugees.

Faced with such a historic responsibility, and at a time when they are the leading economic powers, the United States and Europe have a duty to embark on the energy transition. Yet the treaty clearly states its ambition to develop hydrocarbon trade between the USA and Europe, without imposing any constraints whatsoever. Europe's position is all the more surprising, not to say schizophrenic, given that in 2008, the Commission set itself the target of reducing greenhouse gas emissions by 20% by 2020, increasing energy efficiency by 20% and raising the contribution of renewable energies to 20%.

Without political will, there will be no fight against global warming, and no development of renewable energies and energy efficiency. Of course, the ideal public policy has yet to be found. But it certainly needs to promote these new energies, while at the same time curbing the power of the incumbent energy companies. How can anyone expect us to believe that negotiations between Areva, Exxon or Total will result in a policy that promotes the energy transition? The transatlantic treaty will only strengthen their already dominant positions.

Indeed, TAFTA's other component on investment protection confirms this observation, as any public policy promoting a particular energy by imposing restrictions on another form of energy (such as closing Fessenheim or banning hydraulic fracturing) could be perceived as a barrier to trade, and the companies concerned could challenge them in arbitration tribunals.

Courts Above the Law

The future transatlantic free-trade agreement will include a mechanism for settling investor-state disputes (ISDS). As in previous free-trade agreements, this mechanism is designed to settle commercial disputes between investors and states. It has the distinctive feature of entrusting them to an arbitration body, which means that the dispute is taken out of the hands of national or international courts (the WTO's dispute settlement body, for example, or an international court of justice).

The International Centre for Settlement of Investment Disputes (ICSID) already exists in Washington, set up by the International Bank for Reconstruction and Development (IBRD), to deal with this type of dispute between a State and an investor from another State. Its judges are professors of law or business lawyers appointed on a case-by-case basis (one arbitrator appointed by the investor, one by the State, and the third by the Bank). Appeals are not permitted in this type of proceeding.

There are obvious dangers in this mechanism, as companies could use it to effectively combat collective preferences in the areas of health, food or education, to name but a few. Henceforth, any law, or political choice, can be perceived as an obstacle to corporate investment and be the object of contestation. With this type of mechanism, the commercial interests of companies are legally placed above the preferences of states. And any feedback from experience is bound to reinforce our concerns.

For example, in the context of the free-trade agreement between the United States and Ecuador, ICSID ordered Ecuador to pay Occidental Petroleum $1.77 billion, as Ecuador had terminated a contract with the company for failing to meet its obligations. Cigarette manufacturer Philip Morris used the same procedure in 2010-2011 against the governments of Uruguay and Australia for running anti-smoking campaigns. Investors are increasingly using this type of recourse: in 1999, the number of complaints stood at 11, compared with 45 in 2004 and 62 in 2012. Investor complaints have been upheld, at least in part, in 70% of decisions made public[36]. It should also be noted that when the State wins, unlike multinationals, it receives no financial compensation. It's a risk-free trial (except for a few legal fees) for the investor-company.

---

36. UNCTAD (United Nations Conference on Trade and Development), "Dramatic rise in international investment disputes", Press release, April 10, 2013.

Some would argue that in the case of Europe and the United States, it is already possible to have recourse to this mechanism, and that the number of complaints remains low compared to the 3,200 international investment agreements in force today. It's true that these arbitration tribunals are not systematically called upon, but their existence nevertheless remains a threat, especially in sectors where profits are very high and time is not an important factor[37], as is the case in the energy sector.

In practical terms, the ISDS mechanism would simply extend and amplify the case law developed by the European Union's courts —and even by national administrative courts— relating to the legal certainty of entrepreneurs (and more broadly of economic agents). This right to legal certainty can be expressed as follows: "An entrepreneur is entitled to an economically stable legal environment", and any change to this environment must be compensated.

But unlike the future ISDS, for national and European administrative jurisdictions[38], the right to legal certainty —and therefore to compensation or to the annulment of the (new) binding rule— is assessed according to the legitimacy of the new rule (is it justified on public service grounds? Health? To reduce risks of any kind?) and the cost of the new (unforeseeable) rule to the economic agent suffering its effects (is the prejudice special and abnormal?). The task for the administra-

---

37. According to UNCTAD, the procedural timeframe is no faster than that of a national court.

38. A direct referral by a private individual against a State is now authorized.

tive courts is therefore to develop a doctrine that will enable new rules to be established, while ensuring that the burden of participation in this rule is equitable for all. It is not a question of the courts preventing the establishment of any new rules.

The same will probably not be true of the future ISDS. Especially if it is inspired by the ICSID doctrine, which stipulates that a company has the right to the legal environment it knew when it started its business, and therefore has the right to be compensated for the profit lost by any change in legislation or regulation that is unfavorable to it[39]. In other words, with the introduction of ISDS, it will be impossible, or very costly, for a State or the European Union (but also for the United States) to enact new rules by law or regulation.

In this context, it may come as a surprise that the European Union would agree to include a mechanism of this nature. But a closer look at the economic policies chosen since the beginning of the Union's construction will soften the blow.

Fear of public deficit, debt and inflation has obsessively accompanied the economic construction of the European Union, leading to a disarmament of national sovereignty in budgetary and monetary matters. By depriving European countries, on the one hand, of these two weapons available to all non-European countries, and by choosing competitiveness as its main objective, on the other, the Commission has led countries to play on lower taxes and/or wages. Multinationals

---

39. Such a difference in jurisprudence could be seen in court decisions concerning the exploitation of shale gas in France.

found themselves in an increasingly powerful position to blackmail the fiscal and social conditions of the countries in which they invested. Faced with political choices muzzled by the Commission's criteria, other, far more powerful sovereigns emerged: the financial markets and transnational corporations.

And, in fact, the implementation of the transatlantic treaty, accompanied by special tribunals dedicated to corporate investments, is perfectly in line with previous political choices made by European leaders. After the economic guarantee offered to private creditors through the annihilation of monetary policy, here is the legal guarantee offered to entrepreneurs through the annihilation of the possibility of legislating on labor and consumer rights.

Some will say that France and Germany have already voiced their opposition to the inclusion of such a mechanism, and that a month-long online consultation has been set up by the European Union. But can we believe in this illusion of democracy? How many online consultations have been scorned when it came to the arbitrations of those in power? The risk remains, and experience shows that at European level, whatever the consequences for the people, a mechanism that has been put in place is difficult to undo.

Conclusion

TAFTA presents obvious risks for European and American citizens. We have seen that the economic models used to quantify job creation are largely open to criticism; that negotiations between representatives of multinationals could lead to a lowering of standards that would be detrimental to workers and consumers; that the introduction of arbitration tribunals will make it possible to monitor states so that new rules deemed too protective by multinationals are no longer enacted; and finally that by strengthening the role of incumbent energy companies, the treaty risks making an energy transition even more difficult.

In reality, TAFTA is less an opposition between representatives of the United States and Europe than an opposition between multinationals and citizens. By consolidating their hold, guaranteeing them a legal order that is unfavorable to improving the lives and safety of workers and consumers, but also preventing the fight against the degradation of the planet, the treaty seems to want to organize a new state of capitalism capable of fighting against the evolution of rules. The big winner of this agreement will therefore not be the United States, or even Europe, but global capitalism.

What's more, TAFTA in no way addresses Europe's current problems, nor the planet's challenges, such as the urgent need to protect the environment, regulate finance, increase in inequality and combat extreme poverty. It could even exacerbate these problems.

It's up to all citizens to get to grips with these issues, to debate, to demand accountability, to make the economy a political affair, i.e. a matter for the choices of the city, and to put a stop to an "expertocracy" too often at the service of the strongest. Industrial and financial oligarchies dominate too much and lead people to catastrophe: yesterday the subprime crisis, today TAFTA.

Admittedly, this treaty may seem far removed from our day-to-day concerns, but as the great Italian jurist Piero Calamandrei said in his fight against indifference to politics: "The world is so beautiful, there are so many things to see, to enjoy, rather than worry about politics. Politics is not a pleasant thing. But freedom is like air, and we measure its value when we realize that we lack it[40].

So before the trap closes, let's get the debate going on this treaty and reject a future designed by others.

---

40. Calamandrei (Piero), "Discurso sulla Costituzione" ["Speech on the Constitution"], January 26, 1955.

Table of Contents

Best sellers Max Milo Editions

Hitler's banker, Jean-François Bouchard

Confessions of a forger, Éric Piedoie Le Tiec

The Koran and the flesh, Ludovic-Mohamed Zahed

Governing by fake news, Jacques Baud

Governing by chaos, Collectif

A political history of food, Paul Ariès

Mad in U.S.A.: The ravages of the "American model",
Michel Desmurget

Mondial soccer club geopolitics, Kévin Veyssière

Putin: Game master?, Jacques Braud

Treatise on the three impostors: Moses, Jesus, Muhammad,
The Spirit of Spinoza

TV Lobotomy, Michel Desmurget

9 782315 012640